Called to Love and Leadership

Wisdom Spoken Out From The Inside Of A Miracle

••• •••

Precious Dear

COPYRIGHT PAGE

ISBN: 979-8-9939652-1-5

Library of Congress Control Number: 2026909269

Precious Holistic Touch LLC
www.PreciousHolisticTouch.com

Dedication

To my children,

You have seen me in ways the world never will.

Through cycles…
Through seasons…
Through moments of strength and moments where I was still learning how to stand.

You have watched me love, lead, fall, rise, and find my way back to God again and again.

And my prayer is not that I was perfect before you…
but that I was real.

That you witnessed growth.
That you saw surrender.
That you experienced what it looks like to return to God, even after getting it wrong. I pray that what you have seen in me…
strengthens your own relationship with Him.

That you seek Him first.
That you trust Him fully.
And that you never feel the need to lose yourselves to be loved.

Everything I am becoming…
is for you as much as it is for me.

Foreword

There are moments in life when love feels so real, so present, and so undeniable that you begin to believe it must also be right. This book challenged that belief in me.

Reading Love and Leadership was not easy for me. It required me to sit with truths that I did not always want to face, truths about love, alignment, purpose, and the difference between what feels right and what is right in the eyes of God.

What she shares in these pages is not just her story, it is her obedience.

I watched, in real time, what I now understand more clearly through her words. What I once interpreted as distance, rejection, and emotional withdrawal was actually discipline. What felt like love fading was, in truth, her choosing alignment over attachment.

She loved me. That is something I will never question.

But what she reveals in this book is that love alone is not enough when it pulls you out of alignment with your purpose and your relationship with God. She speaks openly about how loving me, while real, created internal conflict, how operating in a space that looked like commitment without covenant led her into confusion, assumption, and spiritual unrest.

From my side, I felt the shift.

Conversations became less frequent. Time together became limited. Her presence, once open and consistent, became guarded and intentional. Where there was once ease, there was now distance. And if I am honest, it felt like I was being slowly removed from a place I once held in her life.

The moment of truth for me came when I read the words, "I'm single."

We had argued that in many ways before, yet continued on as if we were not. But to read it, to see it in writing, was an understanding that only a fool could ignore. It forced clarity where there had been confusion. And while it hurt, it also healed the place in me that had been so misunderstood while she was making her changes.

What I did not understand then, I understand now. She was not rejecting me. She was choosing herself. She was choosing God.

That kind of choice comes with a cost.

She writes about the discipline it took to remove behaviors that were no longer aligned. She speaks about the impact it had on her children, her identity, and her emotional well being. She acknowledges the grief, not because the love was not real, but because it was not aligned.

Realizing that many people walk away from relationships out of anger, disappointment, or betrayal gave me a different perspective on what I experienced.

This was not that.

She did not walk away because love was absent. She walked away because alignment was missing. She walked away because what we had, while real, was not in order with what she believed God required of her life.

There is a difference.

One is reaction. The other is obedience.

And while one leaves confusion, the other brings clarity, even if that clarity comes with pain.

She also speaks honestly about me, about the weight of my unhealed areas and how they affected her. That was not easy to read, but it was necessary. Growth does not come from comfort, it comes from truth.

What stands out most is her decision to stop performing a relationship and instead honor her identity as a future wife. She chose not to settle into something undefined when she believes God has already defined what is meant for her.

That level of clarity requires courage.

And while this book is written from her perspective, I believe it will speak to anyone who has ever found themselves in a relationship that felt real but left them internally divided. It will challenge you to examine not just who you love, but how you love, and whether that love is aligned with who you are called to be.

For me, this book became more than her story.

It became a mirror.

A mirror that showed me where I was, where I was not, and where I still need to grow.

If you are reading this, understand that this is not a story about love lost. It is a story about love refined, redirected, and surrendered to something greater.

And that kind of love requires leadership.

With that, I want to say I am proud of her. I carry no ill will toward her. My love for her will always be a part of my heart.

I am thankful to know a woman who chose growth over my circumstances, her circumstances, and the adversity of our relationship in order to walk in alignment. That is honorable to say the least.

One thing I know for sure, God will carry her through, as He always has.

Nathaniel Canfall Jr.

TABLE OF CONTENTS

PREFACE:
Before You Read This

God does not provide favor over honoring boyfriends and girlfriends.
Okay, okay… hear me out.

This is not one of *those* books.

I do trust in God, big G, not the little ones, and because of who He is to me, He will be referenced all up and throughout this book. But let me be clear from the beginning…

This is NOT a devotional (as was my first book *7 Days of Fasting for Alignment and Overflow,* available now at www.PreciousHolisticTouch.com).

This is not a neatly packaged, scripture-by-scripture breakdown of life.
This is not written from a place of having it all figured out.

This… is lived.

This is what it looks like to be in the middle of learning, unlearning, healing, and becoming, all at the same time.

Everything you're about to read came from real moments. Real decisions. Real consequences. Real growth. Some of it came through prayer. Some of it came through therapy. Some of it came through heartbreak. And some of it came through God sitting me down and correcting me in ways I couldn't ignore.

What I share in these pages took me over 10 years to learn. Not because I wasn't capable… but because I was out of alignment, trying to force what God had not yet confirmed, and honoring things He never asked me to.

And if I can help you recognize even one thing sooner than I did…
then every lesson, every tear, every moment of confusion was worth it.

This book is not about perfection.

It's about constants.

The truths that remain the same regardless of who you are, where you come from, or what season of life you're in. The kind of truths that don't change based on emotions, relationships, or timing. The truths that transcend dimensions, portals, and planes.

Because one thing I've learned is this:

When we get out of alignment, life gets loud.
Confusing.
Heavy.
Unclear.

But when we come back into alignment; when we seek God first, when we stop performing, when we stop striving to be chosen and instead choose obedience, things don't necessarily become easy…

But they become clear.

This book will challenge you.

It may stretch you.
It may even confront some things you've normalized.

But if you allow it to… it will also free you.

I am not writing this as someone who has arrived.
I'm writing this as someone who answered the call… and is still walking it out.

Still learning how to love.
Still learning how to lead.
Still learning how to do both… without losing myself or putting anything before God.

So, before you turn the page, understand this:

You are not about to read perfection.
You are about to read truth.

And if you're willing to receive it…

It just might change how you see love, leadership, and yourself.

PART I: THE CALLING
(Before Understanding)

Chapter 1: A Lover of Love

I was once told that I was a lover of things…

And at the time, I didn't fully understand what that meant. It sounded light. Almost playful. Like someone noticing that I had a soft spot for beauty, connection, and the little things that make life feel full.

But looking back now… it was deeper than that.

I wasn't just a lover of things.

I was a **lover of love**.

I loved deeply.
Naturally.
Instinctively.

It wasn't something I had to learn, it was something that lived in me. The way I cared, the way I showed up, the way I poured into people… it all came from a place that felt both powerful and effortless. It was second nature.

I didn't just want love.
I wanted to **BE love**.

To live it.
To grow it.
To protect it.
To give it freely.

From a young age, there was always this quiet knowing within me…
that I was called to be a mother, a wife.

Not just in title, but in posture. In spirit. In the way I showed up.

I carried a nurturing nature that extended beyond what was required of me. I wasn't just caring, I was **invested**. I wanted the people around me to feel seen, supported, and safe.

And as life began to unfold, that part of me only grew stronger.

Becoming a mother amplified it.
Stepping into leadership strengthened it.
Taking on responsibility refined it.

I learned how to carry.
How to provide.
How to lead.
How to make things happen, no matter what.

But intertwined in all of that strength…
was still that same woman at her core.

The one who loved deeply.
The one who desired connection.
The one who still believed in the beauty of love.

And somewhere along the way, my **identity** began to root itself in that.

Not just in who I **was**…
but in what I **gave**.

In how I showed up.
In how I loved.

I didn't realize it then… but my desire to love and be loved was becoming one of the strongest driving forces in my life.

It influenced my decisions.
My relationships.
My expectations.

It shaped how I saw myself… and how I believed others would see me.

Because when you are naturally nurturing… when you are wired to love…
you don't question if you should give it.

You give.

Freely.
Fully.
Without hesitation.

And for a long time, I believed that was enough.

That loving well… meant everything would align.
That giving love… would naturally bring love back in the way I desired it.

But what I didn't understand yet was this:

Being called to love…
does not mean you understand how to love **in alignment**.

It doesn't mean you know:

- when to give
- who to give to
- how much to give
- or when to pull back

And it definitely doesn't mean you understand what love requires…
or what it costs when it's given out of order.

I knew I was called to love.

I felt it.
I lived it.
I moved through life from that place.

But I hadn't yet learned that love, real love, aligned love, requires more than feeling.

It requires **timing**.
It requires **boundaries**.

It requires **discernment**.
And most importantly… it requires **God at the center**.

And at that stage of my life…

I had the calling.

But I didn't yet have the understanding.

And that's where this journey begins.

Chapter 2: Built to Lead, Wired to Carry

If I'm honest…
I didn't just become a leader because I wanted to.

I became a leader because **I had to**.

Life didn't really give me the option to sit back and figure things out slowly. From early on, responsibility found me, and once it did, it never really left.

Becoming an unwed mother at 19 shifted everything.

Not just emotionally… but structurally.
The way I moved. The way I thought. The way I made decisions.

It was no longer about me.

It was about making sure everything and everyone around me was okay, no matter what it took.

And from that point on, I stepped into a role that I would carry for years…

Head of household.
Provider.
Protector.
Decision-maker.

Even when I was tired.
Even when I didn't have the answers.
Even when I felt like I was figuring it out as I went.

There was no pause button.

There was only one mindset:

Make it happen by any means necessary.

And I did.

Over and over again.

I learned how to manage everything…
a household, children, schedules, emotions, finances, responsibilities… all at once.

And somewhere in the middle of all of that…
I realized I was good at it. Not just good, but great!

Not just surviving, but **leading**.

That same mindset followed me into my career.

As a young nurse, I didn't just show up to complete tasks, I showed up with care, compassion, and a level of ownership that naturally set me apart. I paid attention. I thought critically. I anticipated needs. I stepped in where others stepped back.

Leadership didn't intimidate me… it felt familiar.

Because I had already been doing it at home.

Managing.
Coordinating.
Making decisions under pressure.
Holding everything together when things felt like they were falling apart.

So, when opportunities for growth came… I stepped into them.

And quickly.

From nurse… to leadership.
From managing patients… to managing systems, teams, and outcomes.

It made sense.

Because I was already wired for it.

But what I didn't realize at the time…
was that the very thing that made me strong…

Was also the very thing that was quietly weighing me down.

Because being built to lead…
and being wired to carry…
are **not** the same thing.

And I had become both.

It was a **blessing and a curse**.

The blessing?

I could handle anything.
I could figure it out.
I could make something work even when it didn't look like it should (clean up woman, I've been called).

I was dependable.
Reliable.
Strong.

The curse?

I felt like I had to do everything.

I struggled to release control.
To trust others.
To allow things to be done differently than how I would do them.

Because for so long… doing it myself was the only way I knew it would get done right.

So, I carried more.

More responsibility.
More pressure.
More expectations.

Even when no one asked me to.

I took it on automatically.

Because that's what I had trained myself to do.

To carry.

To fix.
To manage.
To make sure everything and everyone was okay.

Even at the expense of myself.

And the truth is…

When you live like that long enough, it becomes your normal… Sounding familiar yet?

You don't even question it.

You don't recognize the weight… because you've grown used to holding it.

You don't recognize the exhaustion… because you've learned how to function through it.

You become **high functioning**.

Operating on autopilot.
Moving from one responsibility to the next.
Handling what's in front of you… while already thinking about what's coming next.

From the outside, it looks like strength.

It looks like success.
It looks like you have it all together.

But on the inside…

Your cruise control has turned into hydroplaning, with the wheels spinning on top of the surface beyond your control…

You're carrying more than you were ever meant to hold alone.

And that's where I found myself.

Leading in every area of my life…
but rarely allowing myself to be supported.

Showing up for everyone else…
but not always showing up for myself in the same way.

Because I had learned how to lead out of necessity…

But I hadn't yet learned how to **rest in it**.
How to **share it**.
How to **balance it**.

I didn't yet understand that leadership, when done in alignment, is not about carrying everything…

It's about **being guided**.

But at that stage of my life…

I wasn't just leading.

I was carrying.

And I was carrying it… alone.

And while I thought that strength would serve me in every area of my life…

I was about to learn…

that the way I led… would directly impact the way I loved.

Chapter 3: The Dual Calling Conflict

There came a point where I had to sit with a question that wouldn't leave me alone…

Not in my relationships.
Not in my leadership.
Not even in my quiet time with God.

It followed me.

Pressed on me.

Challenged everything I thought I understood about myself.

The question was simple… but it carried weight:

Can a woman be both soft and authoritative?

Can I be loving… nurturing… gentle…
and still stand firm in who I am as a leader?

Can I be the woman who pours…
and also the woman who leads, directs, and corrects?

Can those two versions of me…
exist without one canceling the other out?

Because for a long time… it felt like they couldn't.

It felt like I had to choose.

Either be:

- soft… or strong
- loving… or respected
- nurturing… or taken seriously

And the truth is… I was both.

Naturally.

That wasn't something I had to force.
It was how I was created.

The best part of being a woman to me, is that I carried a softness… a gentleness… a nurturing spirit that showed up in how I loved, how I cared, how I gave.

But I also carried authority.

A presence.
A voice.
A leadership that didn't ask for permission,

and knew how, when, and where a professional "G Checking" was warranted, via email or in person.

I knew how to step in.
How to make decisions.
How to move things forward.

And while those qualities worked together in some areas of my life…

In other areas, especially in relationships,

They clashed.

There were moments where I felt like my strength was admired…
until it showed up in a way that required accountability.

Moments where my leadership was respected…
until it entered a space where someone expected me to shrink.

Moments where the same traits that made me powerful…
made me "too much" in the wrong environment.

And I found myself asking:

Is it possible for someone to love and admire the leader in me… and not resent her in relationship?

Because I had experienced both.

Admiration… and resistance.
Support… and discomfort.

And it left me confused.

Not about who I was…

But about how I was supposed to show up.

There was also another question that sat heavy in my spirit:

Can I be led… while leading?

That one… required honesty.

Because after years of being the one in control… the one responsible… the one who made things happen…

Letting someone else lead?

Didn't come naturally.

Not because I didn't desire it…

But because I didn't always feel safe enough to release control.

For so long, I had been the one holding everything together.

So even in spaces where I wanted to soften…
where I wanted to be covered…
where I wanted to rest…

There was still a part of me that stayed alert.

Watching.
Assessing.
Ready to step in if needed.

Because I knew what it felt like when things fell apart.

And I refused to let that happen again.

Calling it what it is, I refused to relinquish control.

But that mindset… that survival posture…

Began to interfere with my ability to fully receive love.

Because love, real love, requires vulnerability.

It requires trust.
It requires release.

And those things don't come easy when you've been wired to carry.

So now I found myself in this tension…

Called to love.
Called to lead.

But trying to figure out how to do both… at the same time… without losing myself in either.

And if I'm honest…

There were moments where I questioned if it was even possible.

Because the world will tell you one thing…

Relationships will show you another…

And your experiences will sometimes contradict both.

What I began to realize, through my prayer life, self-reflections, and through lived experience,

Was that the conflict wasn't in the calling.

It was in the alignment.

Because God didn't call me to choose between love and leadership.

He called me to both.

But not outside of order.

Not outside of timing.
Not outside of Him.

NOT outside of His Design.

And that's where I had to pause…

And really ask myself:

Was I trying to force these callings to coexist in spaces where they were never meant to function together?

Was I trying to love…
without alignment?

Was I trying to lead…
without covering?

Was I expecting balance…
in environments built on confusion?

Because when love and leadership are not rooted in God…

They compete.

They conflict.
They **exhaust** you.

But when they are aligned…

They complement each other.

They strengthen each other.
They flow effortlessly.

That understanding didn't come overnight.

It came through experience.
Through discomfort.
Through moments where I had to confront myself, my patterns, and my expectations.

And even then…

I was still learning.

Still processing.

Still trying to figure out what it truly looked like…

To be a woman who could love deeply…

And lead effectively…

Without compromising either.

And that question…

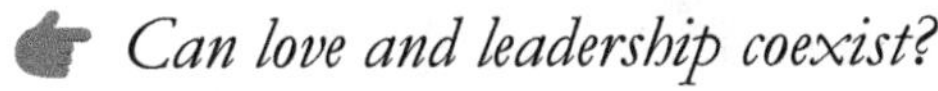

Can love and leadership coexist?

Didn't just start the journey…

It became the very thing that shaped everything that followed.

PART II: MISALIGNMENT (When Love Is Out of Order)

Chapter 4: The Premarital Mindset Without Covenant

I believed we were in a premarital relationship…

Not loosely.
Not casually.
I believed it with conviction.

In my mind, we weren't just dating.
We weren't just "seeing where things go."

We were **working toward marriage**.

That belief shaped how I showed up.

How I spoke.
How I moved.
How I loved.

I wasn't operating as a girlfriend…

I was operating as a **wife in preparation**.

Baby this was a courtship in my eyes.

Or at least… that's what I told myself.

Because the desire to be a wife had always lived in me. I had already come to terms with that. I knew it wasn't random. I knew it was tied to my calling. I knew God had been preparing me, shaping me, stretching me, maturing me…

So, when I found myself in a relationship that *looked like* it had potential…

I stepped into it fully.

Not halfway.
Not guarded.

Fully.

I began to align my actions with what I believed was coming.

I prayed over him.
Covered him spiritually.
Considered his needs.
Adjusted my life, my time, my energy…

As if we were already in covenant.

As if the commitment had already been made.

As if God had already confirmed what I was hoping for.

But the truth was…

We had never come into agreement.

Not fully.

Not clearly.

Not in the way that mattered.

There were conversations, yes.
Moments of hope, kind of.
Statements about the future, of course.

But there was no **mutual understanding** with the foundation in God.

No covering.
No alignment.
No covenant.

And yet…

I moved as if there was.

That's where the misalignment began.

Because while I was showing up with the mindset of a wife…

He, was still navigating life from where he was.

Healing.
Rebuilding.
Recovering.

We were both in transition…

But we were not in the same place so to speak.

Not spiritually.
Not mentally.
Not in timing.

And timing… matters more than we like to admit.

Because two people can feel something real…

And still be out of alignment.

Two people can care deeply…

And still not be on one accord.

Two people can see a future…

And still not be ready to walk into it **together**.

There was no one "right" or "wrong."

But there was a lack of **order**.

And when things are out of order…

Confusion follows.

Miscommunication follows.
Frustration follows.
Disappointment follows.

Because I was trying to function in a role…

That had not been established.

I was carrying the weight of something…

That had not been agreed upon.

I was **honoring** a position…

That God had not yet confirmed.

And the deeper truth?

I wasn't just acting in love…

I was acting in **assumption**.

Assuming that what I felt… was shared equally.
Assuming that what I saw… was seen the same way.
Assuming that what I was preparing for… was already in motion.

But assumptions will have you building on something that isn't stable.

And when reality shows up…

Everything begins to shake, quake, and break, Lord help me.

I remember the moment when that reality became clear.

It wasn't loud or dramatic.

But it was sharp!

I had made a statement, jokingly, lighthearted, yet serious, about the future union; that at my next event, I would reveal my new book cover and it would be my wedding ring.

And the response I received chilled me to the bone.

"We haven't discussed that…"

Because from my perspective…
we *had* discussed it.

Maybe not in one formal sit-down conversation with a timeline and checklist…

But in the in-between moments.
In the late-night conversations.

In the "next year" statements.
In the way we spoke about the future like it was already forming.

There were words exchanged that, to me, carried weight.

There were conversations where marriage was mentioned, and not as a distant idea… but as something that was coming.

So when I heard:

> *"We haven't discussed that."*

It didn't just sound like correction.

It sounded like **denial of something I had already emotionally committed to.**

And that's what made it hit my chest the way it did.

Because in that moment, I wasn't just hearing his words…

I was realizing that what I thought was **shared understanding**…

Was actually **my interpretation**.

I paused.

Not because he was completely wrong…
but because something in my spirit shifted.

My ear had become sensitive. Even as a little girl I had this thing about my ears. I would have heightened moments of sensitivity and a slight gentle ringing that I can't describe.

God had been working on my discernment, answering my prayers for clarity, for truth, for alignment…

And in that moment, through a gentle ringing, I heard more than what was said.

I heard what was **not** there.

Agreement.

Clarity.
Oneness.

It was like everything slowed down long enough for me to check in with myself.

To ask:

Wait… have we really been on the same page?
Or have I been filling in the blanks with what I hoped was true?

Because I had already positioned myself mentally…

As a wife in preparation.

I had already adjusted my posture.
My expectations.
My prayers.

I was speaking from a place of **certainty**…

While he was responding from a place of **present reality**.

And those two things did not match.

That's why it hurt.

Not because he rejected me in that moment…

But because it revealed that I had moved ahead of where we actually were.

And when that realization hits…

It doesn't just touch your mind.

It hits your **heart**.

Because now you must confront the possibility that:

You may have built something… in your mind… that hasn't been fully built in real life.

And that kind of awareness?

It doesn't come gently.

It pierces.

It humbles.

It slows you down.

And in my case…

It stopped me right in my tracks… And by tracks, I mean train tracks, like I was hit by a train while standing on the track.

And in that moment…

Everything slowed down.

Because I had to sit with a truth I didn't want to fully face:

We were not on the same page.

And maybe… we never were.

That moment didn't just reveal miscommunication.

It revealed misalignment.

Because I had moved ahead emotionally, spiritually, and mentally…

Without confirmation.

Without covering.

Without covenant.

And God, in His mercy…

Allowed that moment to check me.

Not to hurt me…

But to **realign me**.

Because the truth is…

God does not bless what He did not establish.

And I had placed myself in a position…

Trying to steward something…

Trying to honor something…

Trying to build something…

That He had not yet confirmed.

Not in that season.
Not in that way.

That doesn't mean the connection wasn't real.

That doesn't mean the love wasn't genuine.

But it does mean…

It was out of order.

And when something is out of order…

It doesn't flow the way it's supposed to.

It feels forced, confusing, and heavy.

Because you're trying to operate in a space…

Without the grace that comes with alignment.

That chapter of my life taught me something that took years to fully understand:

You cannot prepare for a role…

By prematurely stepping into it.

You cannot act as a wife…

Without the agreement, the covering, commitment, and the covenant that comes with it.

And you cannot expect peace…

When you are operating outside of God's order.

I thought I was preparing.

I thought I was being intentional.

I thought I was walking in what God had called me to.

But in reality…

I was living in a role…

That God had not confirmed.

And that misalignment…

Would go on to teach me lessons I couldn't have learned any other way.

Chapter 5: Performing for Love

There is a difference…

Between loving someone…
and performing for love.

And for a long time…

I didn't know the difference.

I know that I'm not alone in this; we can find ourselves taking on an identity outside of what God designed, in attempt to appease someone.

So, outside of God's design…

I found myself listening and noting all of the traits, characteristics, behaviors, and actions that were desirable to the person that I was loving.

I started taking inventory.

What does he value? Okay, me too.
What does he desire? Got that in the bag.
What does he need in a woman? Noted.

And once I had those answers…

I got to work.

Because if this was my future husband…
then I needed to make sure I was what he wanted.

Not realizing…

I was slowly stepping outside of who God created me to be.

He desired a woman that cooked with love…
just like his mother did.

A woman that could bake pies from scratch…
like his older sister.

And I saw the beauty in that.

I admired it.

I respected it.

So naturally…

I decided I needed to become that.

So what did I do?

I went to TikTok.

Looking up southern meals.
Recipes.
"How to make it just right."

Because this was a grown man that liked to eat good…

And if I was going to be his wife one day…

I needed to have this part down pack.

So I started trying.

Cooking meals.
Testing recipes.
Even making videos here and there, like that was my ministry or something.

As if this was just naturally who I was.

And don't get me wrong…

I could cook.

I have children.
Who have favorite meal request every now and then.
I've experienced the joy of feeding my family.

But this?

This was different.

This was me trying to maintain something that wasn't natural to my daily life.

Trying to keep up with cooking 3 to 5 times a week…

On top of everything else I already carried.

And if I'm being honest…

It was exhausting.

I remember one day so clearly.

I'm in between work…

Kids are at school…

And I decide, today is the day.

I'm going to cook.

Log in to Tik Tok, search and find the perfect recipe…

I leave, go grocery shopping, grab all the ingredients.
Entire time I'm in my head spiraling:

Is he going to like it?
Should I tell him I'm cooking?
Or just surprise him once I get the taste right?

I get home…

Start prepping.

Onions sliced.
Peppers cut.
Meat seasoned and marinating.

And right in the middle of that…

I have to stop and go pick the kids up.

Because life doesn't pause.

They get in the car, hungry, of course.

"McDonald's!" is the request.

And I'm tempted…

Because I'm tired already.

But no, I'm locked in.

I've already started.

But also considering the afterschool munchies, which are Beyond any starvation known to man,

So, I grab them something quick, from Mc D's due to the uncertainty of the time it will take for me to finish cooking.

We get back home.

They're eating fast food.

And I'm standing there…

Looking at everything laid out on the counter like:

Okay… lock in.

Because at this point, I'm committed.

So I cook.

Finish the meal.

Sit down.

Taste it…

And it's good.

Like… really good.

So now I'm excited.

I invite him over.

And of course…

He already ate.

Because I didn't say anything earlier.

But he came anyway for morale support lol.

I served him his plate…

Gave me that look of approval.

And in that moment?

I felt accomplished.

Like I did that!

Like, Success, right?

Like… *this is it.*

But what I didn't realize…

Was what it cost me.

The food sat in the fridge.

And eventually had to be thrown out.

Because pizza was my portion to satisfy the appetite of the kids the next day.

Because I was tired.

Because I couldn't keep up with that pace.

Because that wasn't my natural rhythm.

And when you add that up…

And multiply it by all the other things I was trying to take on…

Trying to prove…

Trying to become…

It becomes clear.

I wasn't just loving.

 I was performing.

Performing in the kitchen.
Performing in my time.
Performing in my effort.

Trying to meet a standard that I believed would make me worthy.

Trying to earn something…

That, in truth…

Should have been given freely.

Because real love…

Does not require you to become someone else to receive it.

Real love…

Does not make you feel like you have to prove your value.

Real God ordained love…

Does not demand that you exhaust yourself to be chosen.

But I didn't understand that yet.

So, I kept going.

Kept trying.

Kept stretching myself beyond what God designed for me in that season.

And the truth is…

While I was spending hours:

- searching recipes
- grocery shopping
- cooking meals
- trying to perfect something

I was neglecting something far more important.

The time, energy, and focus…

That was meant to be used for what God actually called me to.

Building.
Growing.
Walking in my purpose.

Because had I truly been seeking first the kingdom…

Had I truly been in alignment…

Everything that was meant for me…

Would have flowed to me.

Effortlessly.

Without performance.

Without anxiety.

Without striving.

But instead…

I was trying to become the wife of my boyfriend's desire.

Instead of being the woman God already created me to be…

For the man He designed for me.

And that right there?

Was the lesson.

I wasn't just cooking meals.

I was trying to earn love.

And love…

Was never meant to be earned.

Chapter 6: Idolizing the Idea of Marriage

It took one session.

One conversation.

One question…

To unravel everything I thought I had in order.

If you haven't already, SIS GET YOU A FAITH BASED THERAPIST! …But not mines because I keep her busy and don't need y'all filling up her schedule when I need her.

I remember it so clearly.

I had been going through the motions, mentally, emotionally, spiritually trying to make sense of where I was in my relationship… why I felt the way I felt… why something still felt off even though, on the surface, everything looked like it had potential.

I was doing what I knew to do.

Praying.
Processing.

Trying to adjust myself.
Trying to be better.

Trying to become what I thought was needed.

And in the middle of that session…

My therapist asked me a question.

Simple.

Direct.

"Have you put him before God?"

And immediately, my answer was…

"No."

Of course not.

Because in my mind… I hadn't.

God was still first.

I prayed.
I fasted.
I sought Him.

So that couldn't be it.

But she didn't stop there.

She asked again…

Just… differently.

"Have you put the idea of marriage above God's timing and planning?"

…

And that question?

Landed differently.

Because now…

I couldn't answer as quickly.

I couldn't respond from habit.

I had to **think**. I considered had I been attempting to manipulate God and call it spiritual war faring on behalf of my "future union?" Was it a mutual understanding between me and this man on our next steps? Is it understood that we are working towards marriage?

I had to **feel**.

I had to be honest.

And when I opened my mouth to respond…

It came out softly, weak, with no power behind it…

Almost like the truth was dragging itself out of me.

"…no."

It landed heavy, like a bomb that shook the room.

The residue of my response lingered for a couple of seconds that felt like forever.. filling the room with silence.

This "no" exposed something I wasn't ready to fully admit.

And in that moment…

Something happened to me physically.

I closed my eyes.

My ear started to tingle… to gently ring.

My right eye winced in discomfort.

A sensation I knew too well.

God was speaking.

Not in words I could hear out loud…

But in a way that I could **feel**.

A knowing.

A download.

A correction.

And I knew…

I needed to listen.

My therapist didn't rush to fill the silence.

She let it sit.

Let it settle.

And then she said something that shifted everything:

"Anything… any person, idea, or thought… that you put before God… becomes an idol."

… She elaborated: "*Something that causes you to question God, to question who He already showed you that you are… it is an IDOL.*"

And just like that…

Everything made sense.

Not in a way that felt good.

But in a way that felt **true**.

Because I realized…

I hadn't just been loving.

I had been prioritizing an outcome.

I had been focused on becoming a wife…

To the point where I began to move ahead of God.

To the point where I began to adjust myself…

Not based on His will…

But based on what I thought was needed to secure marriage.

I had been praying…

But my prayers were centered around a **desired result**.

I had been seeking…

But I was seeking with an **expectation attached**.

And without realizing it…

I had placed the idea of marriage…

Above God's process.

Above His timing.

Above His confirmation.

I thought I was preparing.

I thought I was being intentional.

I thought I was aligning myself for what God had for me.

But in reality…

I was trying to help God do His job.

Trying to map out His will.

Trying to make something happen…

That He had not yet confirmed.

And that's where I had to confront a hard truth:

I was not in a premarital relationship.

Not in the way I believed.

Because a premarital relationship requires:

Agreement.
Clarity.
Direction.
And alignment under God.

And we didn't have that.

Not fully.

Not truly.

So everything I was doing…

The covering.
The praying over him.
The anxiety over being enough.
The effort to meet his expectations…

Was coming from a place of **assumption**.

And deeper than that…

It was coming from a place of **misplaced focus**.

Because instead of being rooted in who God already called me to be…

I shifted.

I started focusing on:

What does he need?
What does he want?
Am I enough?
Can I become what he requires?

And in doing that…

I lost sight of something critical.

If God called me to be a wife…

Then I already possess everything required for the man He has for me.

I don't have to earn it.
I don't have to perform for it.
I don't have to reshape myself for it.

Because the man that finds me…

Will recognize what God has already placed in me.

That session didn't just give me clarity.

It gave me **correction**.

It snatched me out of a spiral I didn't even realize I was in.

A spiral of:

- anxiety
- self-doubt
- overexertion
- trying to prove my worth

And replaced it with truth.

A truth that was simple… but not easy:

Seek God.

Fully.

Wholeheartedly.

Without attaching outcomes.

And trust…

That what He has for you…

Will not require you to abandon yourself to receive it.

From that moment on…

I made a decision.

Not based on emotion.

Not based on fear.

But based on obedience.

I vowed to be 100% me.

To use my gifts boldly.
To stop shrinking.
To stop striving.
To stop trying to earn what God already assigned.

And to trust…

That in **His timing**…

He would make me visible to the one meant for me.

Whether that was the man I was with…

Or someone else entirely.

But either way…

I would no longer place the idea of marriage…

Above God.

Because the truth is…

I didn't idolize a man.

I idolized the outcome.

And God loved me enough…

To correct me before I built my life on it.

Chapter 7: Loving Out of Alignment

Loving out of alignment…

Is one of the most exhausting things I have ever experienced.

Because on the surface…

It can look like love.

It can feel like love.
There can be real care.
Real connection.
Real moments that make you believe…

This has to be it.

But underneath…

Something is always off.

Not always loud or obvious.

But present.

A constant undercurrent of:

Confusion.
Tension.
Emotional imbalance.

And you can't always explain it…

But you can feel it.

For me…

It showed up in how I carried things.

Spiritually.

Emotionally.

Mentally.

Because I wasn't just loving him…

I was covering him.

Praying for him.
Warring for him.
Interceding on his behalf.

Speaking life over his situations.
Standing in the gap for things he was navigating.

Trying to be a source of peace…

In moments where he was still healing, still processing, still rebuilding.

And I did it from a genuine place.

From love.
From care.
From the desire to see him whole.

But what I didn't understand at the time was this:

I was fighting battles that were not assigned to me.

Because there is a difference…

Between praying for someone…

And **covering someone you are not in covenant with**.

That level of covering…

That level of spiritual responsibility…

Comes with alignment.

It comes with agreement.
It comes with order.

And we did not have that.

So what happened?

I became overwhelmed.

Because I was carrying spiritual weight…

Without spiritual covering.

Pouring out…

Without being poured into in the same way.

Standing strong…

While quietly feeling unsupported.

And that imbalance?

Started to show up everywhere.

Emotionally…

I felt confused.

Because there were moments where we felt connected…

And other moments where we felt completely out of sync.

Moments where things flowed…

And moments where everything felt forced.

And I couldn't always make sense of why.

Because in my mind…

We were working toward the same thing.

But in reality…

We were healing in two different directions.

At two different paces.

With two different levels of readiness.

And when two people are not aligned…

Miscommunication becomes constant.

You can say the **same** words…

And hear completely **different** meanings.

You can express yourself clearly…

And still feel misunderstood.

You can explain something perfectly…

And somehow it still turns into frustration.

And I experienced that.

Over and over again.

Conversations that should have brought clarity…

Led to confusion.

Moments that should have built connection…

Created distance.

And it wasn't always because either of us had bad intentions.

It was because we were not operating from the same place.

There were times I felt like I was over-explaining…

Trying to be understood.

Trying to bring peace.

Trying to keep things from escalating.

And in doing that…

I found myself shrinking.

Not fully expressing.
Not fully confronting.
Not fully standing in what I knew was true.

Because I didn't want to cause more tension.

I didn't want to disrupt what I believed we were building.

But the truth is…

> You cannot build something solid… on misalignment.

And the more I tried to hold it together…

The more it revealed the cracks.

I also had to confront something deeper.

Something that didn't just come from the relationship…

But from within me.

Patterns.

Responses.

Triggers.

The part of me that learned, from a young age, to:

Be careful.
Not say too much.
Avoid conflict.
Keep the peace, even at my own expense.

The part of me that would rather adjust…

Than fully stand in truth.

And loving out of alignment…

Pulled that version of me to the surface.

Because when things are not grounded in clarity and agreement…

You start to operate from survival…

Instead of stability.

And yet…

Even in all of that…

I loved him.

Still.

Deeply.

That didn't change.

That's what made it so hard.

Because how do you reconcile…

Loving someone…

And realizing that how you are loving them…

Is not aligned?

How do you continue to show up with care…

While recognizing that something is off at the foundation?

That's when God began to make it clear to me…

In ways I couldn't ignore anymore.

Through conviction.
Through discomfort.
Through moments that forced me to pause and reflect.

That this…

Was not about love being absent.

It was about alignment being absent.

And no matter how much love is present…

If alignment is missing…

Peace will be missing too.

That's the lesson I had to learn.

Not easily.

Not quickly.

But truthfully.

Two people healing separately…

Cannot function as one.

Not in the way I was trying to make it work.

Because oneness requires:

Agreement.
Alignment.
Timing.
And God at the center.

And without that…

You will find yourself:

- overextending
- over giving
- overexplaining
- overcompensating

Trying to create something…

That cannot fully exist in that space.

I thought I was loving him well.

But I was loving…

Out of alignment.

And that made all the difference.

PART III: THE BREAKING

(Reality + Revelation)

Chapter 8: The Breaking Point

The conversation had already happened.

The words had already been said.

And I had already felt the sting of it.

But this…

This was different.

This was the part where it settled.

Because the truth is…

It wasn't just about what he said.

It was about what I finally allowed myself to see.

Over the next few days, I got quiet.

Not distant.

Not withdrawn.

Just… still.

Because something in me was shifting.

And I couldn't move past it the way I normally would.

I am infamous for tabling a conversation, storing it in the back of my mind to be forgotten.

I couldn't explain it away.
I couldn't smooth it over.
I couldn't rush to fix it.

I had to sit with it.

And when I did…

The reality became clear.

Everything I had believed…

Was just that.

My belief.

Not fully agreed upon.
Not clearly established.
Not aligned.

And that realization?

It broke something in me.

Not my ability to love.

But the story I had been telling myself.

Because for years…

10… 11 years…

I had been in his corner.

Riding.

Supporting.

As a friend, a partner, that was promoted to girlfriend.

Loving through the ups and downs.

Showing up when it wasn't easy.

Standing beside him through seasons that required patience, understanding, and grace.

So in my mind…

There was a sense of:

This has to lead somewhere.

There was an expectation…

That all of that time, all of that effort, all of that love…

Would result in what I had been praying for.

What I believed I deserved.

But what I had to face was this:

Time does not equal alignment.

Effort does not equal agreement.

Love does not equal covenant.

Because when I really looked at it…

Not through emotion…

Not through hope…

But through truth…

Our actions told a different story.

The miscommunication told a different story.
The lack of clarity told a different story.
The inconsistency in alignment told a different story.

And I had been overlooking all of it.

Not because I didn't see it…

But because I didn't want to accept what it meant.

I was holding on to what I felt.

What I believed.

What I had invested.

And God was showing me…

That what I felt… wasn't enough to sustain what wasn't aligned.

That's the breaking.

Not loud.

Not dramatic.

But deep.

Because now…

I had to release the idea that:

> Just because I loved well…
> Just because I stayed…
> Just because I showed up…

That it guaranteed the outcome I had been waiting for.

And that hurt.

Not just because of him…

But because I had to confront myself.

Where I ignored signs.
Where I filled in gaps.
Where I allowed time and emotion to convince me…

That we were further along than we actually were.

That was the moment it broke.

Not the relationship.

The illusion that what I believed…

was the full truth.

Chapter 9: The Mirror I Didn't Expect

Prior to the realization from the previous chapter…

I went into therapy thinking I needed clarity about him.

About the relationship.
About what I was feeling.
About why something felt off.

Because even after everything began to settle…

Even after the illusion started to crack…

There was still something in me that couldn't rest.

Something I couldn't fully explain.

That underlying tension.
That emotional uneasiness.
That feeling that something wasn't quite right in the pressure I applied to be loved…

Even before I had the words for it.

And that's the part I had to face.

Because once the truth about *us* became undeniable…

God didn't let me stay focused on him.

He transitioned the moment.

…

And turned the **mirror**.

And if I'm honest…

This part was harder than accepting the truth about the relationship.

Because now…

I was no longer analyzing what happened then.

I was looking at **ME** now.

Up until that point, I had made sense of my experiences as a girlfriend showing up a certain way.

I knew I had been loved.

That had never really been the issue before.

If anything…

I had been loved… *too much.*

I had been the woman that men:

Adored.
Pursued relentlessly.
Put on a pedestal.

The One That Got Away...

To the point where it didn't even feel normal.

There were situations that escalated beyond what love should look like.

Boundaries crossed.
Emotions out of control.
Moments that led to fear… to protection… even to restraining orders.

And while I knew those situations weren't healthy…

Somewhere along the way…

I still associated that intensity with value.

With being chosen.
With being desired.

With **Love**.

So when I found myself in a relationship…

Where I wasn't pedestalized…

Where I wasn't overly adored…

Where I wasn't held to that same intense esteem…

I felt it.

I felt tolerated.

I felt unappreciated.

I felt like something was missing.

And that didn't sit right with me.

Not at all.

So, I brought that into therapy.

Trying to explain it.

Trying to process it.

Trying to make sense of why I felt the way I did.

But instead of getting validation…

I got revelation.

Because as I talked…

As I explained…

As I unpacked what I had experienced in those relationships over the years…

Something deeper started to surface.

Memories, that were buried deep, unthought of, erased from my memory...

Not just from relationships…

But from childhood.

Patterns.

Moments where I felt unsafe, unseen,
Misunderstood.
Like I had to tiptoe around emotions that weren't mine…
but affected me anyway.

Moments where I learned to stay quiet…
to avoid conflict…
to keep the peace… even when I didn't feel safe.

Heavy moments, that created big emotions in a little person.
Emotions and memories that were too big to store.

And as those memories came back…

It didn't feel like reflection.

It felt like breaking, that my mind had forgotten but body remembered.

Because I wasn't just remembering…

I was reliving.

That tight feeling in my chest.
That uneasiness in my body.
That need to shrink… to adjust… to not make things worse.

It was familiar, intense feelings that come with being unprotected, misunderstood, and used vs adored and covered.

And the connection to toxic pedestalized behavior,
Seemingly, easing those emotions.

And it hit me in a way I couldn't ignore:

I have been here before.

Not in the same situation…

But in the same feeling.

And somehow…

I had learned how to function in it.

To move through life carrying that tension…

Without always acknowledging it.

That's when I had to confront something real.

Something uncomfortable.

Something freeing all at the same time:

My mind had been protecting me.

Back then… and even now.

Because sometimes…

When experiences are too heavy…

Too confusing…

Too uncomfortable to fully process in the moment…

The brain does what it needs to do to survive.

It softens it.
It stores it.
It tucks it away.

And then life goes on.

You grow.
You function.
You achieve.
You love.

You envision a future union that your relationship had the "potential" to reach.

All while carrying things…

You haven't fully faced.

Until something happens.

A moment.
A conversation.
A shift.

That removes the fog.

And suddenly… Triggered.

Everything you thought was clear…

Isn't.

That's what this was for me.

That conversation in the previous chapter…

Didn't just break the illusion of the relationship.

It broke the illusion I had been living in.

The illusion that everything was aligned.
The illusion that my interpretation was truth.
The illusion that my patterns weren't affecting my present.

Because now…

I could see it.

How I had learned to:

Tiptoe around reality.
Overextend to keep peace.
Normalize emotional imbalance.
Attach meaning where there was no agreement.

And how I carried that…

Into my relationships.

That's when the deeper revelation came.

Not just about my past…

But about my patterns.

I had been pedestalized before.

I had been overly adored.

I had experienced love that felt extreme...

That wasn't love.

And there was something attached to that.

Not just behavior.

Not just coincidence.

A pattern.

A spirit.

Because how does the same intensity…

Show up in different people?

That's when it became clear:

What you attract…

Reveals what's **attached**.

Not just to them.

But to you.

And that realization?

It broke me.

Because now…

I couldn't just say:

"They did this."

I had to ask:

Why did this feel familiar?
Why did I associate this with love?
Why did I allow it?

And that's not easy.

Because it requires ownership…

Without shame.

Awareness…

Without condemnation.

But it is necessary.

Because healing doesn't happen by avoiding the mirror.

It happens…

When you finally look…

And tell yourself the truth.

Chapter 10: Feel the Feels

After everything surfaced…

After the mirror…

After the memories…

After the realization that what I thought was love had been filtered through unhealed places…

I was left with something I could no longer avoid.

My feelings.

And if I'm honest…

That was the hardest part.

Because I had learned how to function without fully feeling.

Not intentionally.

Not in a way I was aware of.

But over time…

I had **mastered** something that looked productive…

That even sounded healthy when I explained it:

I intellectualized everything.

I could take an experience…

Break it down.
Analyze it.
Understand it.
Find meaning in it.

I could explain why something happened.
Why someone responded the way they did.
Why I felt what I felt…

Without actually sitting in the feeling.

And for a long time…

That worked.

Or at least…

It looked like it did.

Because I was still moving forward.

Still accomplishing things.
Still showing up.
Still producing results.

But what I didn't realize was this:

Just because I accepted something as normal…

Did not mean it was healthy.

My life had been full.

Full of responsibility.
Full of pressure.
Full of highs and highs and more highs…

Even the lows felt like high-functioning survival.

So, my mind and my body…

Adapted.

I learned how to keep going.

How to keep producing.
How to keep showing up.

Even when something didn't feel right.

Even when something hurt.

Even when something needed to be addressed.

And instead of stopping…

I would shift.

Focus on what I could control.
Handle what was in front of me.
Keep moving.

And the feelings?

They got placed somewhere else.

Not gone.

Not healed.

Just… stored.

And this is where the realization hit me in a way I couldn't ignore.

Because in therapy, we talked about what happens when you do that.

When you don't feel the feelings.

When you don't sit with them.
Name them.
Process them.

They don't disappear.

They collect.

Like a cloud.

Everything you didn't feel…

Everything you pushed past…

Everything you told yourself you didn't have time to deal with…

It goes somewhere.

And over time…

That cloud gets heavier.

At first, it's manageable.

You can still see clearly.
Still function.
Still move.

But eventually…

That cloud fills up.

And when it does?

It rains.

And when it rains…

It pours.

And now you're standing in something that feels overwhelming…

Trying to figure out:

Why do I feel like this?
Where did all of this come from?

Not realizing…

It's **everything** you never allowed yourself to feel.

That was me.

And if that wasn't enough…

God gave me another visual.

One I couldn't ignore.

I remember talking about my home.

The heat wasn't working.

So what did I do?

I adjusted.

I got a heater.

Stayed in one room.

Made it work.

Me and the kids…

We were warm.

We were functioning.

We were okay… *in that space.*

But the rest of the house?

Cold.

And the temperature outside?

Dropping, Frigid.

And what happens when pipes sit in the cold too long?

They freeze.

And when they freeze?

They burst.

And when they burst?

Now you're dealing with damage that could have been prevented.

Flooding.
Destruction.
A bigger problem…

From something that was ignored.

And that's exactly what happens…

When you don't deal with what's underneath.

I was functioning in one room of my life.

Handling what I could control.
Keeping things together.

But emotionally?

There were areas I had left cold.

Unattended.
Unaddressed.

And eventually…

That pressure had to go somewhere.

That's what I was feeling.

Not just the present moment.

But the accumulation.

And that's when the truth became clear:

Avoiding emotions delays healing…

But it does not cancel it.

You can push it back.

You can move past it.

You can tell yourself you'll deal with it later.

But later always comes.

And when it does…

It doesn't ask permission.

That's why I had to learn something new.

Something that didn't come naturally to me:

"Feel the feels."

Not just think about them.

Not just explain them.

Feel them.

Name them.

I'm sad.
I'm hurt.

I'm angry.
That didn't feel good.

Identify where it came from.

Why did that affect me?
What did that remind me of?
What did that trigger?

And then…

Address it.

Not avoid it.
Not suppress it.
Not minimize it.

Speak it.

Process it.

Close it out with truth.

Because only then…

Does it stop following you.

I had learned how to lead.

I had learned how to love.

But now…

I was learning how to feel.

And that…

Changed everything.

Chapter 11: When My Daughter Spoke Truth

There are moments in life…

Where the truth doesn't come from where you expect it.

Not from a mentor.
Not from therapy.
Not even from your own reflection.

But from someone watching you…

Closely.

Quietly.

Over time.

For me…

That truth came from my daughter.

We were together, just spending time.

She was going through her younger sister's social media, those little "spam" accounts, messages, posts…

And what started off light…

Turned into something heavy.

Because what I began to hear from her…

Was a reflection.

Not of who I thought I was showing up as…

But of how my life was being **perceived**.

It felt like déjà vu.

Because my youngest daughter…

Had already expressed something similar before.

A resistance.

A discomfort.

A feeling about me being in a relationship.

And now…

My oldest daughter confirmed it.

She said it plainly.

Not disrespectfully.
Not emotionally out of control.

Just… honestly.

"No one is good enough for you."

And while that could sound flattering on the surface…

It wasn't.

Because as the conversation continued…

The truth got deeper.

Sharper.

More specific.

She told me…

She had grown to love him.

But she didn't agree with the relationship.

And then she put the brakes on me:

"You have a type."

That didn't sit right with me.

At all.

Because in my mind…

I wasn't choosing the same kind of men.

I wasn't repeating patterns.

I wasn't accepting anything less than what I deserved.

So I pushed back.

Gently… but firmly.

And that's when she began to explain.

She brought up things I had normalized.

Moments I had minimized.

Situations I had either justified…

Or moved past without fully addressing.

She spoke about arguments…

The kind that happen in front of them.

The tone.
The energy.
The way it made me look…

In her eyes.

"He tries to belittle you."
"He makes you sound uneducated."
"You can explain something perfectly… and he'll still 'mansplain' it."

And she said it plainly:

"I don't like it."

And then…

She said something that went even deeper.

"We see you as strong… beautiful… intelligent… kind… loving…"

And in that moment…

I didn't feel proud.

I felt exposed.

Because now I had to sit with something I wasn't prepared for:

My daughters were watching me…

And forming their understanding of love…

Through what I allowed.

And it felt like something got stuck in my throat.

Too big to swallow.

Too heavy to ignore.

Because I had to ask myself…

A question that shook me:

Am I leading well at home?

What type of role model am I? What example am I setting?

Not in my career.

Not in my business.

Not in the community.

But where it matters most.

Because how could I speak to young women…

About love and leadership…

If my own daughters were questioning what they were seeing?

How could I lead others…

If I hadn't fully mastered…

Or even recognized…

The patterns in my own relationships?

That moment didn't just make me reflect…

It made me question everything.

Life as I had previously known it...

My choices.
My standards.
My awareness.

And for a moment…

I felt like I had failed.

Not just as a woman…

But as a mother.

Because in trying to love…

In trying to figure it out…

In trying to navigate life…

I may have exposed them to things…

That didn't reflect what I was teaching.

And that's a hard place to sit in.

Because now it's not just about your healing.

It's about what your unhealed places have shown to others.

Especially your children.

And in that moment…

I couldn't run from it.

I couldn't explain it away.

I couldn't soften it.

I had to receive it.

Even though it hurt.

Even though it challenged me.

Even though it made me uncomfortable.

Because truth…

Even when it comes from your child…

Is still truth.

And that day…

I realized something I will never forget:

Leadership doesn't start on a platform.

It starts at home.

And sometimes…

The most honest reflection you'll ever receive…

Is from the ones who've been watching you the whole time.

PART IV: THE AWAKENING

Chapter 12: December 2025 — My Yes to God

It didn't happen all at once.

It wasn't one big moment where everything just made sense, and I walked away feeling completely whole.

It was a process.

A breaking…
A revealing…
A sitting in truth longer than I was comfortable with.

But there was a moment…

A real moment…

Where everything shifted.

December 2025.

I can't even describe it as just a thought.

It was an experience.

An encounter.

Because after everything I had gone through…

After the conversations…
After the therapy…
After the realizations…
After the mirror…

I reached a place where I could no longer pretend.

I could no longer hold on to what I wanted things to be.

I could no longer operate from assumption, hope, or emotional attachment.

I had to face **truth**.

Fully.

And truth will humble you.

Because now…

It wasn't about him.

It wasn't about the relationship.

It wasn't about what could have been.

It was about me and God.

And where I stood with Him.

I had to acknowledge something that didn't feel good to admit:

I had been out of alignment.

Not because I didn't love God.

Not because I wasn't praying.

Not because I wasn't seeking Him.

But because I had allowed my desires…

To move ahead of His direction.

I had tried to shape something.

Define something.

Hold onto something…

That He had not confirmed.

And once that became clear…

I had a decision to make.

Not emotionally.

Not based on what I felt like doing.

But spiritually.

Was I going to continue doing things my way…

Or was I going to fully surrender to His?

And surrender…

Is not as soft as it sounds.

Because surrender means letting go.

Letting go of:

What you thought it would be.
What you planned for it to be.
What you hoped it would become.

It means releasing control.

And control…

Had become familiar to me.

As a leader…

As a mother…

As someone who had spent years making things happen…

Letting go of control?

Didn't come naturally.

But…

I knew I couldn't move forward carrying both.

My will…
and
God's will.

So, **I gave Him my yes.**

Not a halfway yes.

Not a "yes, but…"

A real yes.

"God, whatever You say… I will do."

"However You want this to go… I will follow."

"Even if it doesn't look like what I wanted… I trust You."

And that kind of yes…

Changes everything.

Because now…

You're no longer trying to figure it out on your own.

You're no longer forcing outcomes.

You're no longer holding onto things out of fear.

You're allowing your steps to be ordered.

That's when things became clear.

Not perfect.

Not easy.

But clear.

I understood that I was not in a premarital relationship.

Not in the way I had convinced myself.

I understood that certain things…

Certain actions…

Certain levels of access…

Were not mine to operate in.

Not without covenant.

Not without agreement.

Not without God at the center.

And once I saw that…

I couldn't unsee it.

So I made changes.

Not always perfectly.

Not always easily.

But intentionally.

I began to pull back from things that didn't align.

Not always explaining first.

Not always being understood.

And that caused its own set of emotions.

Hurt.
Confusion.
Even feelings of abandonment; from his perspective.

But this time…

I wasn't led by emotion.

I was led by obedience.

Because when God makes something clear…

You don't get to negotiate it.

And that's the part people don't talk about

Obedience can feel lonely.

Especially when it requires you to:

Move differently.
Love differently.
Show up differently.

But I had reached a point where I understood something deeply:

Being in alignment with God…

Was more important than being understood by people.

So I stayed in the Word.

I fasted.
I prayed.

Not for the relationship to work…

But for me to remain aligned.

For my business.
For my calling.
For the assignment God had given me.

And as I did that…

Something began to shift.

Not outside of me first…

But within me.

Peace.

Not because everything was resolved.

Not because everything felt good.

But because I was no longer fighting God.

That was my awakening.

Alignment doesn't come from control.

It comes from surrender.

And in that moment…

I finally chose it.

Chapter 13: Philippians 4 — The Blueprint

After my yes…

After choosing alignment over control…

I still had one question sitting with me:

What does this actually look like?

Because it's one thing to say yes to God.
It's another thing to live it out, daily, consistently, in real situations.

Especially when you are called to both love and lead.

I remember that night so clearly.

I had just finished signing books.

Preparing. Reflecting. Sitting with everything that had been unfolding in my life.

I grabbed my Bible before laying down, just to read, to center myself.

I went to Proverbs 4:23… a scripture I had been meditating on:

"Guard your heart…"

Because at that point, I knew my heart needed guarding.

But as I was reading, I saw the note…

That led me to Philippians 4.

And when I turned there…

It wasn't random.

It was **answer**.

Because what I had been wrestling with....

How to be soft and strong
How to love and lead
How to not lose myself in either

Was laid out right there.

It hit me so clearly, almost like it was spoken directly to me:

"Let your gentleness be evident to all."

That was the first part.

Because I had been trying to figure out:

How do I remain soft…
without being taken advantage of?
How do I love…
without losing authority?

And the answer wasn't to harden myself.

It was to remain gentle.

Not weak.

Not passive.

But grounded.

Controlled.

At peace within myself.

Then it continued:

> *"Do not be anxious about anything…"*

That one…

That one checked me.

Because anxiety had been present in ways I didn't fully acknowledge.

Wondering if I was enough.
Wondering if things would work out.
Wondering if I was doing the right thing.

But the instruction was clear:

Do not be anxious.

Not because life is perfect…

But because God is in control.

"…but in every situation, by prayer and petition, with thanksgiving, present your requests to God."

That's where the exchange happens.

Instead of carrying it…
You give it to Him.

Instead of overthinking it…
You pray about it.

Instead of trying to control it…
You trust Him with it.

And then came the promise:

"And the peace of God, which transcends all understanding, will guard your hearts and your minds…"

That was it.

That was the answer.

Peace.

Not control.

Not perfection.

Not everything going how I wanted.

Peace.

A peace that doesn't make sense.

A peace that doesn't depend on circumstances.

A peace that allows you to stand in the middle of chaos…

And still be grounded.

That became my first anchor:

#1 A Peaceful Perspective

Because if I could maintain peace…

I wouldn't be pulled into anxiety.
I wouldn't be reactive.
I wouldn't be easily shaken by what others were experiencing.

I could love from peace.

I could lead from peace.

And I realized something important:

Don't allow others to pull you into their storm…

Pull them into your peace.

That changed everything.

Then I kept reading.

"Whatever is true, whatever is noble, whatever is right, whatever is pure, whatever is lovely, whatever is admirable, if anything is excellent or praiseworthy, think about such things."

And that was the second part.

#2 A Praiseworthy Mindset

Because how you think…

Shapes how you show up.

If my mind is focused on:

What's wrong
What's missing
What's frustrating

Then that's what I will reflect in my love…

And in my leadership.

But if my mind is anchored in:

What is **true**
What is right

What is pure
What is admirable

Then I lead from a place of excellence.

Then I love with intention.

Not ignoring reality…

But choosing perspective.

Because this doesn't mean you don't address issues.

It means you don't allow negativity…

To be your foundation.

And that's what I had been missing.

I had been trying to figure out how to balance:

Being loving
Being assertive
Being understanding
Being firm

When the answer was never in switching between the two.

It was in anchoring both…

In peace and truth.

Because when you lead from peace…

Your authority doesn't feel aggressive.

When you love from truth…

Your softness doesn't feel weak.

It flows.

That's when I understood:

Peace is the bridge between love and leadership.

And once I had that…

I no longer had to choose between the two.

I just had to stay anchored in Him

Chapter 14: Boundaries, Obedience, and Letting Go

Once I understood the blueprint…

Once Philippians 4 became real to me, not just something I read, but something I could **live**;

I didn't have the luxury of staying the same.

Because revelation requires response.

I couldn't keep saying I wanted peace…

And still entertain what disrupted it.

I couldn't say I trusted God…

And still move based on my feelings.

I couldn't say I was aligned…

And continue operating in things He had already made clear were out of order.

So now…

It was time to move.

Not emotionally.

Not reactively.

But **obediently**.

And obedience…

Looks different when it becomes real.

Because it's not just about what you start doing.

It's about what you stop allowing.

That's where the boundaries came in.

Not loud boundaries.

Not aggressive ones.

But clear.

Intentional.

Non-negotiable.

I had to start cutting off behaviors…

That didn't align with what God had shown me.

Not because they were easy to walk away from, they aren't.

Not because I didn't still feel connected, I still do.

Not because love wasn't still there, It is.

But because I finally understood:

Love without alignment will keep you in cycles.

So I began to pull back.

From things that felt familiar…
but weren't right.

From conversations that blurred lines.
From access that hadn't been earned through covenant.

From patterns that I now recognized…

As out of order.

And I didn't always explain it first.

That was hard.

Because I'm a communicator.

I like clarity.
I like understanding.
I like to make sure everyone is on the same page.

But obedience doesn't always come with full explanation.

Sometimes…

You move because God said move.

And that can feel uncomfortable.

For you.

And for the other person.

Because now…

The dynamic changes.

What was once considered normal in the relationship…

Is no longer allowed outside of God's covenant for man and wife.

What once felt easy…

Now feels restricted.

What once flowed…

Now requires discipline.

And that shift?

It brings up emotions.

Hurt.
Confusion.
Even feelings of rejection or abandonment…

From the other side.

And if you're not careful…

You will be tempted to go back.

To make it easier.

To smooth things over.

To return to what feels familiar.

But I had to remind myself:

Familiar does not mean aligned.

And not Aligned right now, doesn't mean Never.

So I stayed the course.

Even when it felt uncomfortable.

Even when it wasn't fully understood.

Even when I felt the pull to go back to what I knew.

Because this time…

I wasn't choosing based on feelings.

I was choosing God.

And that meant redefining the relationship.

Not from what I hoped it would be…

But from what it actually was.

No longer speaking as if we were already becoming one.

No longer operating in roles that had not been established.

No longer giving *access* that required covenant.

That was the hard part.

Because letting go…

Doesn't always mean walking away completely.

Sometimes it means…

Letting go of the version of it you created in your mind.

Letting go of the expectation.
Letting go of the timeline.
Letting go of the outcome.

And choosing to see it for what it is.

Not what it could be.

And that kind of letting go?

Requires strength.

Because your feelings don't always agree.

There were still moments where I cared.

Still moments where I felt connected.

Still moments where I had to remind myself:

Just because I feel it… doesn't mean I follow it.

That was new for me.

Because for a long time…

I had been led by what I felt.

By what made sense emotionally.

By what I could justify in my mind.

But now?

I was being led by obedience.

And obedience will **stretch** you.

It will take you out of what feels comfortable…

And place you in what is **correct**.

It will ask you to trust…

When you don't fully understand.

To move…

When you don't have all the answers.

To let go…

When part of you still wants to hold on.

But what I gained in that process…

Was something I had been searching for all along.

Clarity.

Not confusion.
Not overthinking.
Not emotional back and forth.

Clear.

Because when you align with God…

Things may not always feel good…

But they make sense.

That's when I learned:

Obedience will cost you comfort…

But it will give you clarity.

And for the first time…

I chose clarity.

🌷 PART V: THE BECOMING (UNFINISHED ON PURPOSE)

Chapter 15: Called to Love… Myself

After the boundaries…

After the obedience…

After letting go of what I thought it was supposed to be…

I was left with something I had avoided for a long time.

Me.

Not as a mother.
Not as a leader.
Not as someone showing up for everyone else.

Just me.

And if I'm honest…

That was unfamiliar.

Because for so many years…

My identity had been tied to what I did.

What I carried.
Who I showed up for.
How I loved others.

I knew how to pour.

I knew how to give.
I knew how to be there.
I knew how to hold things together.

But sitting with myself?

Without distraction…
Without responsibility pulling at me…
Without a relationship defining part of my identity…

That felt different.

And it revealed something I had to face:

I had been loving others…

Better than I had been loving myself.

Not intentionally.

Not in a way I was aware of.

But in the way I showed up.

In the way I poured out.
In the way I stretched myself.
In the way I made space for others…

While slowly abandoning parts of me.

Because loving others had become natural.

But loving myself…

Correctly…

Required intention.

It required me to ask:

Do I honor myself the way I expect others to?
Do I speak to myself with kindness?
Do I show up for myself… the way I show up for everyone else?

And the truth?

Wasn't always yes.

Because somewhere along the way…

I had learned to find validation in what I gave.

In how I was received.
In how I was chosen.
In how I was valued by others.

And when that shifted…

When I was no longer operating in the same patterns…

When I was no longer performing, overextending, or trying to earn love…

It forced me to confront something deeper.

Who am I…

Without external validation?

Not as someone's partner.
Not as someone being chosen.

But as a woman…

Fully standing in who God created me to be.

That's where the identity shift happened.

Not overnight.

Not perfectly.

But intentionally.

I had to learn how to:

Sit with myself.
Be honest with myself.
Care for myself.

Without attaching it to anyone else.

Because the truth is…

If I don't know how to love myself correctly…

I will always look for someone else to complete that work for me.

And that's not sustainable.

That's where self-abandonment begins.

When you:

Overextend to be accepted.
Shrink to maintain connection.
Adjust who you are… to keep someone else comfortable.

And I had done that, all of it.

In ways I didn't fully recognize at the time.

But now?

I was aware.

And awareness changes everything.

Because now I had a responsibility.

Not to go back.

Not to repeat patterns.

Not to lose myself in love again.

But to rebuild…

From a place of truth.

To love myself the way God loves me.

Without condition.
Without performance.
Without needing to prove anything.

To honor who I am.
To protect my peace.
To stand fully in my identity…

Without shrinking it to fit into someone else's expectation.

And that required me to remove something:

External validation.

Not completely.

Because we are human.

We appreciate being seen.
We appreciate being valued.

But it could no longer be my source.

Because when validation becomes your source…

You will do anything to maintain it.

And I was no longer willing to do that.

Because I finally understood:

You cannot lead others…

From a place of self-abandonment.

And if I was truly called to love…

And to lead…

Then it had to start here.

With me.

Chapter 16: Single, Stripped, and Still Called

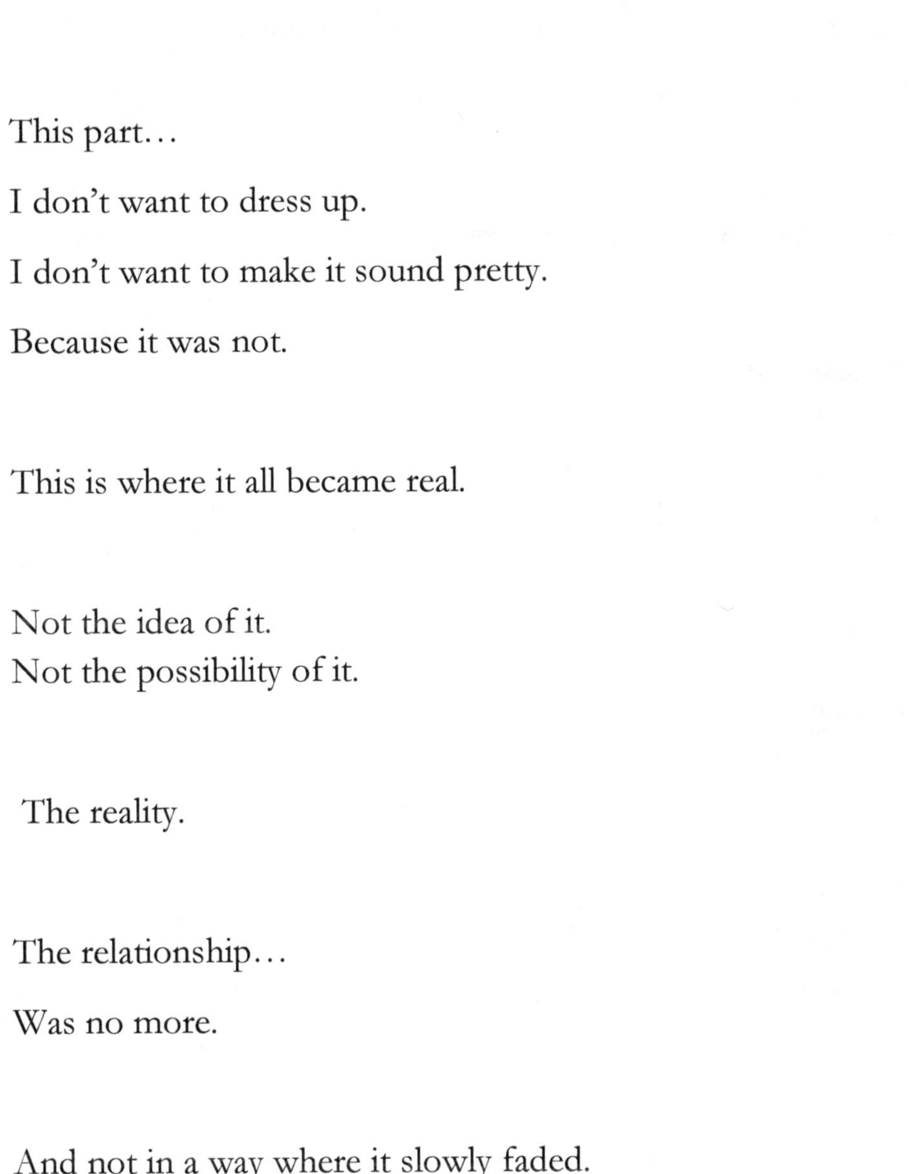

This part…

I don't want to dress up.

I don't want to make it sound pretty.

Because it was not.

This is where it all became real.

Not the idea of it.
Not the possibility of it.

The reality.

The relationship…

Was no more.

And not in a way where it slowly faded.

Not in a way where we both agreed and walked away peacefully.

But in a way where clarity settled in so deeply…

That there was nothing left to hold onto the same way.

And I had to face something I had not faced in a long time.

I was single.

Not just physically.

But mentally.
Emotionally.
Spiritually.

No confusion.
No "we'll see."
No comfort in thinking…

We're still something.

Nothing.

And that kind of realization?

It will take the wind out of you.

Because for so long… YEARS

Whether things were good or bad…

There was always a sense of:

I have someone.

Even if it wasn't perfect.

Even if it wasn't aligned.

It was familiar.

And now?

Silence.

And if I'm honest…

That silence was loud.

It echoed.

Because now I had to sit with a version of myself…

I didn't fully recognize.

A version of me that wasn't:

Trying to make it work
Trying to understand
Trying to be chosen

Just…

Me.

And I didn't know her like I thought I did, at all.

That was the identity crisis.

Not in who I am at my core…

Because I know who I am.

I know **whose** I am.

But in how I saw myself…

Outside of everything I had attached to my identity.

Because for years…

There had always been something tied to it.

A relationship.
A connection.
A "we."

And now…

There wasn't.

And that truth?

Made me want to shut down.

There were moments I wanted to scream.

Moments I wanted to cry until I couldn't feel anything.

Moments I wanted to bury my face in the pillow and just stay there.

Because it hurt.

Not just the ending.

But the realization of:

Time.
Energy.
Love.

Everything I had poured into something…

That didn't become what I thought it would be.

And that brought up something I wasn't prepared for:

Grief.

Real grief.

Not just over him…

But over the version of life I thought I was walking into.

The marriage I thought was coming (literally have a wedding dress pointlessly sitting in my closet to this day).
The future I had envisioned.
The comfort I had created in my mind.

Gone.

And grief doesn't ask for permission.

It's disrespectful, it shows up when it wants to.

In the calm of the middle of the day.
In random moments where your mind slows down just enough…

To **feel** it.

And I felt it.

At the same time…

Life didn't stop.

Even when I wanted it to.

And that was the part that made it even harder.

Because while I was grieving…

I still had to show up.

For my children.

For my home.
For my responsibilities.

For my calling.

Work didn't pause.

The pressure didn't lift.

If anything…

Everything intensified.

I was navigating changes at work…

Unrealistic expectations.

A shift in responsibilities that I didn't ask for.

Travel demands.
Time constraints.
Mental exhaustion.

At the same time…

My body didn't feel like my own.

Medication changes.
Anxiety.
Mood shifts.
Weight in places I didn't recognize.

I didn't feel like myself.

And yet…

I still had to be present.

For my 3 children.

Who needed discipline.

Who needed guidance.

Who needed a mother…

That I didn't always feel equipped to be in that moment.

Because I was trying to hold everything together…

While feeling like I was coming apart inside.

And in the middle of all of that…

One thought kept trying to creep in:

Maybe I'm not called to this.

Not to love.
Not to lead.

Maybe I got it wrong.

Maybe I'm supposed to be alone.

Maybe I should just focus on myself and leave everything else alone.

Because how can I lead…

When I feel like I'm failing in areas of my own life?

How can I speak to love…

When I'm grieving it?

That thought…

Was **heavy**.

But even in that…

God didn't release me from my calling.

And that's what I had to come to terms with:

Calling doesn't pause…

Just because life hurts.

It doesn't stop because you're grieving.

It doesn't go quiet because you're confused.

It doesn't disappear because you're uncomfortable.

It continues.

Even when you don't feel ready.

Even when you don't feel strong.

Even when you don't feel like yourself.

And that's where I found myself.

Broken…
Grieving…
Uncomfortable…
Unsure…

But still called.

And that's a hard place to stand.

Because now…

You're not moving from strength.

You're moving from obedience.

And sometimes…

obedience looks like showing up…

while you're still healing.

Chapter 17: Leadership Before the Platform

Right in the middle of all of that…

The grief.
The pressure.
The identity shift.
The uncertainty.

God didn't pause my assignment.

If anything…

He confirmed it.

Because while I was trying to make sense of what was breaking in my personal life…

There were things unfolding in my calling…

That I could not ignore.

My first conference.

And I remember…

Standing in that space of belief and obedience…

Trusting God for something I had never done before.

All while in this foreign season of my life.

But God downloaded the vision and walking in obedience was my portion. It's all I had for direction when all around me was darkness and I can't see the way.

So, trusting that where He was guiding me, He would provide.

I was praying.

Discerning.

Believing God for a venue that would match the vision He gave me.

The first option?

Too expensive.
Would have taken a large portion of my non-existent budget.

The second?

Booked for months out.

And I could feel disappointment trying to creep in.

But I remembered something that had been spoken to me…

Advice that stayed with me:

Don't force what God is redirecting.

So instead of panicking…

Instead of rushing…

I paused.

I prayed.

I trusted.

I kept searching.

I found another location.

One that stood out to me more than the others.

I sent the email inquiry…

And decided I would follow up in the morning.

Simple.

That same evening…

7:00 PM.

Virtual Bible study.

And at 7:28 PM came around, while still in Bible Study…

I received a text.

"Check into the eau Claire Rooney building…. It's one decent size room, an entrance way , and a full kitchen …. You honestly can make that room whatever you want to it's an open space …. We have had plenty of thing there… and I know it's available be we were going to use it that same day for our family party we just changed locations".

My eyes swelled with tears, chills were sent through my body, the hairs stood up on the back of my neck.

I had not shared that I had emailed that same location earlier at 5:38pm!

That it was the location I really wanted but was nervous and doubting if I would be able to get enough women registered to fill it!!

My GOD! I didn't have to chase this.

I didn't have to force this.

I didn't even name it out loud to the person who texted me.

And yet… the space was released and My name was waiting.

That's not accidental timing, that's orchestrated provision.

What this told me about the event itself;

If the venue came together like this…

If the timing aligned without manipulation…

If the door opened before I knocked…

Then the impact of the gathering will carry that same grace.

Women will come who weren't on the original list.

Conversations will happen that weren't on the agenda.

Healing will take place, that no speaker could script.

Scripture calls this moment confirmation through two witnesses.

While I was studying the Word, the Word answered me.

I didn't strive for confirmation.

Confirmation interrupted my study.

This is love and leadership together:

Loving God enough to trust Him in the unseen,

And leading well enough to move when He opens the door.

That night, I learned again that when God assigns a vision, He also assigns the space, the people, and the timing.

Sometimes the answer doesn't come from heaven.

Sometimes it comes through a text message

while you're already sitting at His feet.

Adding to how good God is, when I finally saw the room, I realized God hadn't just provided a venue,

He had prepared an atmosphere.

The space fit the assignment.

And to think..

God went ahead of me.

And the space?

Was already waiting.

Aligned and Ready.

That moment…

I saw something clearly:

While I was questioning myself…

While I was grieving…

While I was trying to figure out if I was even worthy to lead…

God was still trusting me with the assignment.

He didn't withdraw it.

He didn't pause it.

He didn't wait for me to feel better.

He confirmed it.

That's when I understood:

Leadership doesn't start on a platform.

It starts in private.

In obedience.
In trust.
In moments where no one else sees what God is doing.

Because when God assigns something…

He also confirms it.

And this time…

I didn't have to force anything.

I just had to follow.

Chapter 18: Love Is Not What I Thought

After everything I had just experienced…

After seeing God move the way He did, without force, without striving, without me having to prove anything.

I had to sit with a truth that felt both simple…

And completely new to me.

Love… is not what I thought.

Because for so long…

The way I understood love had been shaped by:

Experience.
Emotion.
Effort.

Love looked like showing up.
Love looked like proving.
Love looked like staying.
Love looked like doing whatever it took to make it work.

And in some ways…

That felt right.

Because I am a lover.

Naturally.

But after everything God had just shown me…

I couldn't ignore the contrast.

Because what I experienced with Him…

Didn't require any of that.

I didn't have to:

Convince Him.
Earn from Him.
Perform for Him.
Prove to Him that I was worthy.

It was given.

Freely.

Fully.

Without condition.

And that's when it hit me…

That's **love**.

Not the kind that exhausts you.

Not the kind that keeps you questioning.

Not the kind that makes you feel like you're always trying to measure up.

But the kind that is stood up in truth.

Agape love.

The kind of love that God gives.

The kind of love that doesn't shift based on performance.

The kind of love that doesn't require you to lose yourself to keep it.

And I had to be honest with myself.

I had not been operating from that understanding.

Because if I was…

I wouldn't have been striving the way I was.

I wouldn't have been overextending.

I wouldn't have been trying to earn something…

That should have been freely given.

And I wouldn't have been accepting…

Versions of love…

That required me to abandon parts of myself.

Because real love…

Does not require you to disappear.

It doesn't ask you to shrink.

It doesn't ask you to prove your worth.

It doesn't ask you to carry what was never assigned to you.

It aligns.

That's the word that changed everything for me.

Alignment.

Because love, when it is aligned…

Flows.

It doesn't feel forced.

It doesn't feel confusing.

It doesn't leave you constantly questioning where you stand.

It makes sense.

Not because it's perfect…

But because it's in order.

And that's what I had been missing.

I had been trying to love…

Without alignment.

Trying to build…

Without foundation.

Trying to give…

Without making sure what I was giving to was right.

And God, in His love for me…

Showed me the difference.

Not through punishment.

Not through rejection.

But through example.

Through how He covered me.

Through how He provided for me.

Through how He made things happen…

Without me having to force it.

And that shifted something in me.

Because now…

I no longer desired love that required performance.

I desired love that aligned.

Love that allowed me to be fully who I am.

Love that didn't compete with my calling.

Love that didn't make me question my worth.

And just as important…

I had to learn how to give love that way too.

Not from a place of overexertion.

Not from a place of trying to secure something.

But from a place of wholeness.

Because when you love from wholeness…

You don't lose yourself.

You don't abandon your standards.

You don't silence your voice.

You show up fully.

And that's when I understood:

Love is not performance…

It's alignment.

And once you experience it that way…

You can never go back to anything less.

Chapter 19: I Already Had It

After everything…

The breaking.
The mirror.
The alignment.
The understanding of what love truly is…

There was still one more revelation.

One that didn't come from a sermon.
Didn't come from a book.
Didn't come from anything external.

It came in therapy.

And it was simple.

So simple…

That it almost frustrated me when I heard it.

"You already have everything you need."

And I remember sitting there like…

No… I don't.

Because at that point in my life…

It didn't feel that way.

I felt like I was missing something.

Missing clarity.
Missing direction.
Missing stability in certain areas.

And if I'm honest…

There was still a part of me that felt like:

Maybe I need to become more… to receive more.

More disciplined.
More structured.
More this.
More that.

But what my therapist said next…

Shifted everything.

"Who you were… before life happened… is who you really are."

And that landed.

Because I had to think back.

Before the responsibilities.
Before the heartbreak.
Before the pressure.
Before the trauma.

Who was I?

Not who I became to survive.

Not who I adapted into to manage life.

Who did God create me to be… from the beginning?

And as I sat with that…

Something softened in me.

Because I realized…

I hadn't lost myself.

I had just been covered.

Covered by experiences.
Covered by responsibilities.
Covered by survival patterns.

But underneath all of that…

I was still there.

The woman who loves deeply.
The woman who leads naturally.
The woman who is intuitive, discerning, and full of vision.

That didn't disappear.

It just got buried.

And life has a way of doing that.

Because as time passes…

Things happen.

Experiences shape you.
Situations stretch you.
Trauma impacts you.

And without realizing it…

You begin to move further and further away from your original design.

Not because you chose to…

But because you had to survive.

And survival will have you:

Adjusting.
Adapting.
Becoming who you need to be…

To make it through.

But healing?

Healing is not about becoming someone new.

That's the part that shifted everything for me.

Healing is about returning.

Returning to yourself.

Returning to truth.

Returning to the version of you…

That existed before the layers were added.

Because God didn't create you incomplete.

He didn't forget to give you something.

He didn't leave out a piece you need to go find.

He equipped you.

From the beginning.

With everything required…

For your life.
For your calling.
For your purpose.

And what life does…

Is attempt to distort that.

To make you question it.
To make you forget it.
To make you believe you have to earn it.

But the truth is…

You already have it.

That's what I had to come back to.

Not striving to become…

But remembering who I've always been.

Not searching outside of myself…

But reconnecting with what God already placed within me.

And that changed how I saw everything.

My gifts.
My voice.
My calling.

Because now…

I wasn't trying to build from lack.

I was operating from wholeness.

And that's a different kind of confidence.

Not loud.
Not performative.

But grounded.

Because when you know…

That everything you need is already in you…

You stop chasing.

You stop forcing.

You stop comparing.

And you start walking.

In alignment.

In truth.

In purpose.

Because the journey was never about becoming someone else.

It was about remembering who God created me to be… all along.

Chapter 20: The Continuation

If you've made it this far…

You might be expecting an ending.

Something that ties everything together.
Something that feels complete.
Something that says:

"And now everything makes sense."

But that's not what this is.

Because this…

Is not the end.

And if I'm honest…

I don't want it to be.

Because what I've come to understand through all of this,

The love.
The leadership.

The breaking.
The awakening.
The becoming…

It doesn't end.

It unfolds.

There is no final version of me…

That has arrived.

No place where I can say:

"I've mastered this."

Because as long as I'm living…

As long as I'm growing…

As long as I'm walking in purpose…

I am becoming.

And that has been the most freeing realization of all.

Because for so long…

I thought there would be a moment where everything clicked.

Where I would feel fully ready.
Fully healed.
Fully confident in every area of my life.

But that's not how this works.

There are still days…

Where I have to choose alignment.

Still moments where I have to check myself.
Still seasons where I am stretched in ways I didn't expect.

There are still parts of love…

That I am learning.

Still layers of leadership…

That are being revealed.

And I'm okay with that now.

Because I no longer measure my growth…

By perfection.

I measure it by alignment.

Am I listening to God?
Am I moving in obedience?
Am I staying true to who He created me to be?

That's what matters.

Not whether I have it all figured out.

Not whether everything looks how I once imagined.

Because the truth is…

Some things are still unfolding.

My story…

Is still being written.

There are prayers I've prayed…

That I haven't seen the full manifestation of yet.

There are desires that still sit in my heart.

There are promises I believe God will fulfill…

In His time.

And this time…

I trust Him.

Not just when things are clear.

Not just when things feel good.

But fully.

Because I've seen what happens when I try to control it.

I've lived what it feels like to be out of alignment.

And I've experienced the peace that comes…

When I let go.

So, wherever you are…

In your journey of love…
In your journey of leadership…
In your journey of becoming…

I want you to know this:

You don't have to have all the answers.

You don't have to rush the process.

You don't have to force anything into place.

You just have to align.

Align with truth.
Align with God.
Align with who you were created to be.

And trust…

That everything meant for you…

Will meet you there.

Because this isn't the end.

It's the **continuation**.

Meet The Author

PRECIOUS DEAR

Nurse Leader • Holistic Practitioner • Founder • Author

Precious Dear is a Nurse Leader, Holistic Practitioner, and nearly twenty-year Registered Nurse dedicated to restoring wellness in the lives of individuals, families, and communities. With a blended background in clinical leadership and holistic care, she serves as both the CEO of Precious Holistic Touch LLC and the Founder of Precious Holistic Touch Foundation Inc., where she equips others with tools for mental, emotional, spiritual, and environmental healing.

Guided by faith and anchored in obedience, Precious has lived and witnessed the power of healing, alignment, and breakthrough in her own life. Her testimony is one of restoration through surrender, learning firsthand that when God orders your steps, overflow follows. Through seasons of sacrifice, caregiving, motherhood, leadership, and personal reinvention, she has embraced the truth that "It's All Connected." Every experience, every struggle, and every triumph becomes part of the assignment God has placed on her life.

As a holistic wellness advocate, Precious is passionate about transforming how people care for themselves, not only physically, but spiritually and emotionally. She empowers youth, supports communities, and uplifts families through education, mentorship, and intentional connection. Her work with the Precious Holistic Touch Foundation Inc. reflects her lifelong mission to cultivate healthy, whole, purpose-driven lives.

In addition to her professional and community impact, Precious is completing her Master of Science in Nursing, Specializing in Leadership and Administration, continuing her journey as a lifelong learner and servant leader. Her calling is woven through every facet of her life, mother, caregiver, mentor, nurse, and woman of faith, and her purpose is to create spaces where others can experience clarity, healing, alignment, and abundance.

Through her writing, coaching, teaching, and ministry, Precious reminds the world that God is still in the business of ordering steps, restoring hearts, and releasing overflow. Her life is a testament to the beauty of obedience and the transformative power of saying "yes" to God.

Connect with Precious

www.PreciousHolisticTouch.com